TREND
BOOK

To Andrew Thomson

ELEVENTH HOUR

Jodie Rankin
Illustrations by Hilary Jackman

Cheshire/Ginn

This book is copyright
and reproduction of the
whole or part without the
publisher's written permission
is prohibited
© 1975 Ian Falk and Bettina Bird
First published 1975
by Cheshire Publishing Pty Ltd
346 St Kilda Road, Melbourne
Also at Sydney, Adelaide, Brisbane
Perth, Wellington and London
Distributed in the UK by
Ginn and Company Ltd
Aylesbury, Bucks
Set and designed in Australia
Printed in Hong Kong by
Dai Nippon Printing Co. (HK) Ltd

National Library of Australia
Cataloguing-in-Publication data

Rankin, Jodie
  Eleventh hour/ [by] Jodie Rankin;
  Illustrations by Hilary Jackman.—
  Melbourne: Cheshire/Ginn, 1975.—(Trend
  books).
  For children.
  ISBN 0 7015 1685 2.

1. Readers. I. Title. (Series).

428.62

Eleventh Hour

Trend level T6

Chapter 1

Kids save their money for all kinds
of things. Surfboards or bikes.
Fishing rods or stamps or knives.
But I don't save my money
for any of those things.
I save my money for birds.
And don't get me wrong—
I mean birds with feathers and wings.
I don't mean girls.

But while we're talking about girls,
I'll tell you about Trixie.

She is one girl-type bird
who liked my budgerigars
as much as I did.
Tell anyone else that you kept an aviary
full of birds and they'd laugh like mad.
But not Trixie. She didn't laugh.
And if *you* want to have a good laugh,
have it right now.
Because the rest of this story
is dead serious.
And 'dead' is just what Trixie
could have been.

I had some pretty good budgies
at the time I'm going to tell you about.
The yellow ones were the best.
Trixie liked the yellow budgies
most of all. But I had blue ones too.
And grey ones.
I had some of the usual green ones
as well. In fact, I had between fifty
and sixty budgies in my aviary.

Anyway, it was because of this interest
in birds that Trixie and I got caught up
in a whole lot of trouble—
smuggling, and some other things as well.
The whole story is still hard for me
to believe, though it's true enough.

Chapter 2

Trixie lives next door to us.
Our houses are two of a set
of five terrace houses.
I kept my birds in an aviary
in the back yard.
It's not a big yard, but it's big enough
for a huge, knotty old apricot tree,
some grass, and my aviary.

One day I was in the aviary,
cleaning it out,
when Trixie stuck her head
over the side fence.
'Having fun?' she asked.

'Terrific!' I said, and grinned.
'So good that you should come
and help me.'

'Wow!' Trixie said. And she laughed.
'It really must be good fun.
I'll come over and give you a hand.'
She climbed up on the side fence
and jumped over.
I watched her walk up to the aviary.

I'd never felt quite easy with girls
until I met Trixie.
But Trixie is different.
She is easy to talk to,
but she doesn't expect you
to keep chatting away all the time.
We can be together for ages
without saying a word—
just cleaning out the aviary,
or standing around watching the budgies.
Or even just sitting doing nothing.

Trixie is as tall as me,
and a bit on the skinny side.
Her long hair is a nothing kind of colour
and she has a habit of tossing it
away from her face.
But it was that grin of hers
that got me right from the start.
It isn't a smile. It's a real grin.

On the day that I was telling you about,
she walked up to the aviary.
She gave me her special grin.
'What now?' she asked.

'Pass me the hose,' I said.

I opened the aviary door just a bit.
The hose was lying outside the door.
Trixie picked it up and passed one end
through the opening.

'Turn on the water. Just a bit,' I said.
Trixie turned on the water.
'Just right,' I said. 'Thanks.'

'Nothing to it,' Trixie replied.
'I just *love* taking orders.'

'Gee, I'm sorry,' I said.

I *was* sorry, too.
Sometimes I say things
and they don't come out the way
I mean them at all.

But Trixie just laughed.
'You've got something on your mind,'
she said. 'I can tell.'

She was right, of course.
'What do you want first—the good news
or the bad news?' I asked her.

'Hmm. The good news.'

'I'm getting some new birds.
Big birds. Parrots.'

Trixie's eyes lit up.
'That's great!' she said.
'So what's the bad news?'

'I'm selling all these budgies
so I can buy the parrots.'

Trixie's face fell.
'Not *all* of the budgies,' she said.
'Not the yellow ones as well. Not them!'

'All of them,' I replied.
'I won't have the money or the room
for the parrots if I don't sell
all the budgies.' I went on hosing out
the bottom of the aviary, but I knew
Trixie was looking at the yellow budgies.

'Well,' she said at last.
'I guess you've made up your mind.'

'I have,' I said.
'I saw an ad in the paper yesterday.
It was put in by Evergreen Aviaries.
I rang up and talked to a man
called Lumsden—Mr Lumsden.
He said he'd make me a clean swap.
All my budgies for some parrots.
They're really special, those parrots.
Dad's taking me to Evergreen Aviaries
tomorrow.'

'Where are they?' Trixie asked.
'Evergreen Aviaries, I mean.'

'At Chelsea. It's a long way,
but it's the only place
with the kind of parrots I want.
I did ring some other places.
But, no go.'

Trixie didn't say anything for a minute.
She stood in front of the aviary,
watching the yellow budgies.
Then she said,
'Could you take a hitch-hiker along
with you tomorrow?'

I knew what she was getting at.
'I was hoping you'd come,' I said.
'Dad wants to leave just after lunch.
About two o'clock. OK?'

'I'll be right on time,' she said.

Chapter 3

On Sunday we left right on two o'clock.
I'd put all the budgies
in some travelling cages I'd made.
The cages took up all the back seat,
so Trixie had to sit in the front
of the car with Dad and me.

It was a beautiful sunny day,
and the traffic was heavy.
You'd have thought
the whole of Melbourne was out
for a Sunday afternoon drive.
What with the heat and the traffic,
Dad was in a real huff
by the time we got to Chelsea.

We pulled up outside Evergreen Aviaries.
'You and Trixie go in,' Dad said.
'I'll sit out here and cool down a bit.
And don't be too long.
It's going to take hours to get back home
through that traffic.'
He lit a cigarette and leaned back
in the seat.
Trixie and I took the cages
out of the car.
Trixie carried the cage of yellow budgies.

Mr Lumsden turned out to be a real creep.
He was very tall, and his shoulders
seemed all hunched up.
He acted kind of funny
the whole time we were there—
as if his mind was on something else.
He was rude too.
You wouldn't have thought
he wanted to sell any birds.

He looked my budgies over.
'Hmm,' he grunted.
'They'll do.'

'Do?' Trixie said. 'Do?
I should just think they would do!
Why, these yellow ones . . .'

But Lumsden cut her short.
'Look, girlie,' he said.
'These budgies are OK. But that's all.
Now come and choose which parrots
you want. I haven't got all day.'
We followed Lumsden out to the aviaries.
Trixie was glaring daggers at his back.
She hates being called 'girlie'.

Mr Lumsden's aviaries were well set out.
And his parrots were great.
I could have stayed there for the rest
of the day, just watching them.

But with the mood Dad was in,
I knew we'd have to hurry.

I chose a pair of Rosellas.
Then I looked at a King Parrot.
Beautiful, it was. Bright red and green.
'Gee,' I said.
'I'd love a pair of those.'

'You would!' Lumsden muttered.
'I've only got that one bird now.
It's a male. I'm waiting for some more
to come in—males and females.'

Right then I knew I wanted a pair
of King Parrots. I said I'd take
the male bird he had, and order a female.
Lumsden made a note of that
in his order book.
He took my name and phone number,
and said he'd ring me
when the female King Parrot arrived.
Great.

The drive home was awful.
Heat. Traffic. Noise.
And Dad in a rotten mood.
I hoped the parrots would live
through it all. They did.

At last we got back home.
Dad headed straight for a cold beer.
Trixie and I headed straight
for the aviary. We let the birds out
in the aviary.

But the aviary still looked
empty somehow.
That morning there had been
fifty-five budgies in there.
Now there were just three parrots.
But those parrots were terrific.
Their colours were really fantastic.
And Trixie had to say that they seemed
a fair swap for all the budgies.
Even the yellow budgies.

So that was Sunday!
And that was the day that started
all the trouble.

Chapter 4

The Friday after I bought the new birds
was cold and wet.
That's Melbourne! One day it is hot
and sunny,
the next it is cold and wet.
The rain fell in a steady drizzle.
After school, Trixie was helping me
to clean out the aviary, as usual.
I heard the phone ringing inside the house.
I knew Mum was out shopping,
and Dad wasn't home from work yet.
I handed the hose to Trixie
and ran inside.

I grabbed the phone. 'Hullo.'

A soft voice answered.
'Is that Mr McNeil? Mr Erle McNeil?'

Right away I knew something was wrong.
Hardly anyone rang me,
and when it did happen,
I always knew who it was.
But I didn't know that voice.
I didn't answer,
so there was a long silence.

'Er . . . I want to speak to
a Mr Erle McNeil,' the voice said at last.
'Is he there, please?'

While I was wondering if I should say
that I was Erle McNeil,
the voice spoke again.
But louder this time.
'Is Mr Erle McNeil there, please?'

I took the plunge.
'I'm Erle McNeil,' I said.
'Who's speaking, please?'

The voice didn't answer my question.
Instead it said, 'You wanted a parrot.
A female King Parrot. Is that right?'

Whew! It's only creepy old Mr Lumsden
from Evergreen Aviaries, I thought.
'Have you got the bird?' I asked.

There was another silence.
Then the voice spoke again.
Only this time it wasn't soft at all.
It sounded . . . well, sort of commanding,
I guess.
'It's not quite like that, son,'
the voice said. 'Now listen.
There's nothing to be worried about.
I'm an officer from the Fisheries
and Wildlife Department.
I'm ringing from our head office.
We'd like to come and have a talk
with you. We have your phone number
here, in Mr Lumsden's book.
But there's no address.
Could we have your address, please?'

A government department! And ringing me!
I broke out in a cold sweat.
'Hey! What's all this about?'
I said into the phone.

'We'll talk about that when we get there.
Your address, please?'

I gave our address.
I mean, you can't fight
a government department.

'We'll be over there in about
half an hour,' the man on the phone said.
'We'll talk things over then.'

We both hung up.

I stood by the phone.
Talk things over!
What things?
What could the Fisheries and Wildlife
Department want with me?

Just then, Mum came in the front door.
Trixie came in from the back yard, too.
She was wondering where I'd got to.

I told them about the phone call.
'Well, let's hope they don't get here
until your father gets home,' Mum said.
'He'll know what to do. I hope.'

Chapter 5

Dad got home just before the men
from the Fisheries and Wildlife
Department arrived.
And Dad didn't know what to do.
Mum was wrong about that one.
Anything to do with
a government department,
and my dad seems to go to pieces.

Two men arrived.
There was a young man
called Mr Patterson.
With him was an older man
called Mr Hicks.
Mr Hicks did most of the talking.
He seemed quite a nice chap, really.

I'll spare you all the details
of what happened next.
Like Mum getting in a flap
and making cups of tea.
And Dad saying, 'Well . . er . . .',
and, 'Yes, but . . .'

I'd broken the law. That sums it up.
The parrots I'd got from Lumsden
were protected birds.
You couldn't keep them unless
you belonged to a special bird club.
The Avicultural Society of Australia,
it's called. I'd never heard of it.

And to top it off,
Mr Hicks said he would have to take
my new parrots away.
That really made me mad.
And I'd just got those parrots!
Swapped all my budgies for them.

Now I'd have no birds
and no money to buy any more. Great!

I just stood there and looked at Hicks.
I felt all twisted up inside.
I didn't seem to be able to speak.

Trixie spoke, though.
'You can't take Erle's parrots away!'
she said to the two men.
'You can't!
He's paid for them. They're his!'

'Sorry, young lady,' Mr Hicks said.
'But we *have* to take them.
We'd be breaking the law too,
if we didn't. It's our job to look after
all protected birds and animals
in this country, you know.
But there's something else
I have to ask you about.'

Hicks looked at each of us in turn.
'Do you know where Lumsden is?'

'What do you mean?' I asked.
'I thought he was still at Chelsea.'

'Well, he's not,' said Mr Hicks.
'He's gone. Disappeared. And we want him.
We want him badly.
We think he's been smuggling birds
out of this country.
We don't know for certain,
but we're pretty sure.
Smuggling birds is a million dollar
racket, you know.
And we think that's what
Lumsden's been up to.'

'Smuggling!' I said.
I just couldn't believe it.

'But who would buy the birds?'
Trixie asked.

'Overseas collectors,' Mr Hicks told her.
'They will pay hundreds of dollars
for just one of our birds.'

'But how could he smuggle big birds
like parrots without anyone hearing
them squawk?' I asked.

'That's where the cruel part comes in,'
said the young man—Mr Patterson.
'They drug the birds.
That puts them to sleep
and stops them making any noise.
Then they pack them in secret
compartments in suit cases or boxes.
You'd be surprised the tricks
these smugglers get up to.
Often the birds are packed so close
together that they can't even breathe.

Then they send them off by air
to overseas countries. Like Singapore.
Hundreds of birds die on the way, though.
It's bad. And it's our job
to stop these smuggling rackets.'

Mr Hicks spoke up then.
He looked at Trixie and me.
'You two kids know what Lumsden
looks like, don't you?'

I said, 'Yes. He's very tall.
He's a real creep too.
I don't think I'll ever forget
what *he* looks like.'

'Well now, I want you to keep your eyes
open for him,' said Mr Hicks.
'We've got one or two of his other
customers on the look out for him too.
We think he will try to skip the country.
If he hasn't already gone.
Will you help us?'

I looked at Hicks and Patterson.
I was thinking about my parrots.
These men were going to take them away.
Why should I help them?
'Well . . . I don't know,' I said.
'I seem to be the loser all round.
Lumsden takes my budgerigars,
 then you take my parrots.
It's just not fair.'

The two men looked at each other.
'It's hard,' said Mr Hicks.
'We know that. But this is our job.
And it's the law.
But it's Lumsden who is to blame
for all this trouble, son. Not us.
We've *got* to catch this man.
Now, will you help us?'

I saw their point. But gee!
It's hard to build up a collection of birds
and then have it taken away from you
just like that. But I said,
'I guess I'll help if I can.
What else *can* I do, anyway?'

'OK. And thanks,' Mr Hicks said.
'Let us know if you see or hear
anything of Lumsden.
You can ring the Department if you do.'
He stood up. So did Patterson.
'We'd better catch these parrots now,'
said Mr Hicks. 'Your aviary, son—
is it out the back?'

'Yes,' I said.

The men got a net and a cage from
their car.
Dad showed them where the aviary was.
I stayed in the living-room with Trixie.
I couldn't watch the men take my birds.

'Lumsden!' I muttered.

'That creep, Lumsden!

If only I could get my hands on him!'

Chapter 6

'Now listen, Erle,' Trixie said to me.
'You can't just sit around the house
all day and mope.
But I know how you feel. Really I do.'

'Hmmph!' I grunted.

'Look,' Trixie said.

'It's been over a week now.

And you've just moped around

the whole time.

Now what about coming into the city.

I've got to get a birthday present for Mum.

I haven't got a clue what to get her.

You could help me. Come on.

What do you say?'

I looked up at Trixie.

'Well . . . I guess you're right,' I said.

'But it does take a bit of getting over.

It's the same as if a kid's new bike

had been stolen, or his surfboard,

or even his car.

OK. Let's go into the city.'

Trixie grinned.

It was a Saturday morning.
Trixie and I caught the bus.
The city was so crowded you could
hardly move. But getting away from home
made me feel better somehow.

After dragging me through
two big department stores, Trixie found
something for her mother's birthday.
A scarf. An orange sort of scarf
with a wavy blue pattern over it.
'That's just what Mum needs
to go with her new outfit,' Trixie said.

'Great,' I said. 'Now let's grab a quick coke
before we catch the bus home.
There's a shop round the corner
where we can sit down, too.
My legs are killing me.'

Trixie grinned at me.

'Thanks for helping me get the present,'
she said.

'And I bet you're feeling better.'

'I am,' I said. 'Thanks to you.'

We were just about to go round the corner
when Trixie stopped me.

We were standing outside a shop window.
It was a travel agency.
There was a huge poster in the window.

JET YOUR WAY TO SINGAPORE—
EXCITING GATEWAY TO THE EAST.

And there was a colourful photograph
of some men in strange-looking hats
sailing around in odd-looking boats.

'Singapore!' Trixie said.
'Those men from Fisheries and Wildlife
said Mr Lumsden might be sending
his birds to Singapore.'

'That's right,' I said.
'And I wouldn't mind betting
that Mr Lumsden is in Singapore right now!
The creep! Come on. Let's get that coke.'

We had just turned to go round
the corner, when BANG!
A man came out of the travel agency
and ran right into us. A tall man.
He had a big coat on, and dark glasses.
Well, he did have dark glasses on
until he ran into us. But they fell off
and rattled on to the ground.

Trixie was knocked over.
I was just going to help her to get up
when I realized who the man was.

It was Lumsden.

He bent down,
snatched up his dark glasses,
and put them on again.
Then he stood up and walked off
into the crowd. His hands were deep
in the pockets of his big, brown overcoat.

It only took a second.
And in that second I seemed to be frozen—
only able to watch him. Lumsden!
Right here in Melbourne—
coming out of a travel agency!

Trixie scrambled to her feet
without my help.
'Who did that?' she said angrily.
'The silly mug!'
But I didn't answer her. I was still
watching Lumsden making his way
along the crowded street.

Trixie saw me gazing into the distance.
'Hey! What's got into you?' she said.

I grabbed her arm. 'Listen!
That man who knocked you down, he's . . .'

'He's a rotten mug! No one can just . . .'

'Trixie! Listen! It was Lumsden!'

Trixie's eyes opened wide.
'You're kidding!' she said.

But I was already dragging her
into the crowd.
I knew I mustn't lose sight of Lumsden.
I could still see his head in the crowd.
It was just as well he was so tall.

'Come on, Trixie,' I said.
'I don't think he recognized us.
We've got to follow him.'

Lumsden was walking fast.
It was hard to keep up with him.
'Where do you think he's heading?'
Trixie asked. She was puffing.

'I don't know. But if he keeps going
this way, we'll end up
at the railway station.'

Lumsden stopped at a corner to wait
for the lights to turn green.
Trixie and I stopped well behind him.
'If he came out of a travel agency,
do you think . . .?' Trixie started to say.

I guessed what she was thinking.
'Yes. I think he's just got a ticket
to fly to Singapore.
I bet he's waited for the last week or so
until things cooled off.
That's why he's been hiding.
Now he's going to skip the country.'

'And he could even be going today,'
Trixie said. 'Erle, we'll have to let
the men from Fisheries and Wildlife know.'

'We can't,' I said. 'It's Saturday.
They don't work on Saturdays,
as far as I know.'

'Well, a cop then.
We'll have to find a cop.
We'll have to follow Lumsden
and look for a cop at the same time.'

'Would a cop believe us?' I asked.
'I mean it does sound kind of way out.'

'It's the only thing we can do.
Can you think of anything better?'

'No,' I said. 'I can't. Keep a look out
for a cop. There should be lots of them
around on a Saturday.'

Just then the traffic lights changed.
Lumsden was off.
Boy! Could he walk fast!
By the time we got to Flinders Street,
my legs were ready to drop off.
Trixie was puffed out. So was I.
And the only cop we saw was on
traffic duty. A fat lot of hope
we had of getting him to help us!

We were just following Lumsden
into Flinders Street railway station,
when a thought hit me.
'Hey, Trixie,' I said.
'How much money have you got?
If he's going to catch a train,
we'll have to buy tickets.'

'Ooo-er!' Trixie said.
'I haven't got much, after buying
Mum's present. Let's see . . .'

She opened her bag and looked inside it.
Then she grinned. 'There's one thing
about my bag,' she said.
'There's always some money in the bottom.
We'll have enough.'

'Well, just make sure you keep enough
for a phone call,' I told her.
'I bet we'll need to make a call sometime.
God knows *where* we'll end up today.'

Chapter 7

People pushed and shoved.
They bumped us. They shouted.
They talked. For a moment we thought
we'd lost Lumsden in the crowd.
Then I saw him again.
He was heading for a ticket office.
Trixie and I battled through the crowd,
our eyes fixed on the back
of Lumsden's big, old brown coat.

At the ticket office, we were right
behind him. We *had* to be. We had to know
which train he was catching.
And where he was going.

'Single to Coburg,'
I heard Lumsden mutter.

The ticket officer slid a ticket
on to the counter. Lumsden paid for it
and picked up the ticket.
Then he turned away, and I moved up
to the counter. I hunched my shoulders
and kept my head down, hoping Lumsden
hadn't seen me. I remember thinking
that it was just as well Trixie and I
were dressed in jeans and jackets.
We looked like most of the other kids.
'Two singles to Coburg,' I said softly
to the ticket officer. Lumsden was still
too close for me to speak any louder.

'Eh?' said the ticket officer.
'Speak up, kid. I can't hear you.'

'Two singles to Coburg,' I said,
louder this time.

I glanced around, but Lumsden was making
his way towards the gates
and on to the station. I grabbed the tickets
and paid for them with Trixie's money.
She was right behind me as I moved away
from the ticket office.

'Lumsden's gone through the gates,'
Trixie said. 'We'd better hurry.
I don't think he's noticed us, Erle.'

I'd been worrying
whether Lumsden had recognized us
when he knocked Trixie over
outside the travel agency.
But I still didn't think he had.

Then Lumsden got into the train
for Coburg. We followed.
Lumsden sat at one end of the carriage
and we sat at the other.

There were a lot of people in the carriage
but we could still see Lumsden.
He kept glancing at his watch.
He glanced round the carriage
from time to time too.
Once he seemed to look straight at us,
and Trixie and I grew uneasy.
We tried not to look at him.

I sat hunched up in the corner seat
with Trixie close beside me.
We had our heads down as if we were
talking quietly to each other.
But I could see Lumsden
out of the corner of one eye.

At last he stood up, ready to get
off the train. The train pulled into
Coburg station and stopped.
Lumsden got out. Trixie and I waited
until the train was just about
to take off again before we got out
of our seats and jumped off the train.

Lumsden was quite a long way in front
of us now, but we had to stay well behind
him so he wouldn't see us.

Up the railway ramp we went,
then along the main street.
Lumsden turned one corner, then another.
And another.
By now, Trixie and I were quite lost.
We didn't know Coburg at all.

There was a house on the next corner
with a bit of a garden.
Round it was a low, red brick fence
with a hedge behind it.
When Lumsden turned that corner,
we had to run so that we didn't lose him.

We peered round the corner
with the red brick fence and the hedge.
There was Lumsden—right in front of us.

He had stopped walking.
He was standing with his back to us,
leaning through the window of a taxi.
He was talking to the taxi-driver.

Trixie and I stopped still.
'Get back,' Trixie whispered to me.
'He hasn't seen us. Quick!'

We found we could still see Lumsden
through gaps in the hedge.

Lumsden pointed to the house—
the one we were standing near.
So that's where he had moved to!
We had found his hiding place.

Lumsden was still talking
to the taxi-driver,
but we couldn't hear much.
Then he took something out of his pocket.
It looked like a piece of paper,
but it wasn't very big.
Lumsden looked at it. Then he said
something to the taxi-driver,
and put the paper back in his pocket.

The driver took out a cigarette
and lit it. Lumsden walked quickly
into the house on the corner.
The taxi waited.

Chapter 8

'Erle,' Trixie said.
'I think Lumsden is on his way
to Singapore right now.
I think that was an airline ticket
he had in his hand.

'Yes,' I said. 'And he's gone
into the house to get his things.
Suitcases and stuff.'

'And I bet there'll be some sleepy parrots
in them, too,' Trixie said.
'Erle, what are we going to do?'

We had to think— and we had to think fast.
'A telephone!' I said.
'We could ring the police.
Did we pass a telephone?'

'No,' Trixie said. 'And anyway,
the police would never get here in time,
even if we could get to a phone.
Lumsden is leaving right now!
I'm sure of it.'

Then I had a wild idea.
It wasn't only wild, either.
It was dangerous too.
Very dangerous.
But anything seemed worth a try then.
Anything?

What I had in mind really was
a desperate move.
But this was the eleventh hour—
the last chance.
The very last chance.

'Trixie,' I said. 'I've got an idea.
It's dangerous, but I think it's
our only chance. Now listen to me . . .'

Trixie listened. And as I told her
my idea, her eyes opened wider and wider.
'No, Erle,' she said. 'You can't do that.
You might get hurt. And anyway,
what could I do with Lumsden on my own?'

'But it's a good idea,' I said.
'It would work. I know it would.'

But Trixie shook her head.
'No,' she said.
'You're not going to do it.
I am.'

'But . . . but it's dangerous!' I stammered.
'You could get hurt!'

'I know,' she said. 'But what's good
for you is good for me. Anyway, I'm a girl.
They'll feel more sorry for me
than they would for you. And you'd have
more chance of holding on to Lumsden
than I would if he tries to make
a break for it.'
Trixie grinned her special grin.
'Well, I'm going to do it,
and that's that,' she said.
'It should work, and besides,
it might even be a bit of fun.'

'Fun!' I said. 'It's not my idea of fun!'

'Well, I'll get ready,' Trixie said.
'I'm going to use Mum's birthday present.
I hope it doesn't get torn or anything.'
Trixie untied the present—
the orange and blue scarf.
She tied it tightly round her head,
then tucked all her hair into it.

Suddenly Lumsden came out of the house.
He was carrying some suitcases.
'I wonder how many birds he's got
in those,' I said.

'Hmm,' Trixie muttered.
'Anyway, I'm ready. You tell me when.'

'OK,' I said.
'Wait till the taxi is just pulling away.'

The taxi-driver jumped out and helped
Lumsden to put his cases in the car.
Then they both got into the taxi.
The driver started the motor.

'Right,' I said to Trixie.
'Are you ready?'

'Ready as I'll ever be,' she said.

'Well . . . good luck,' I said to her.

'Thanks,' Trixie said, and she smiled.
'I'll need it.'

Then I saw the driver put the car
into gear. The car started to move off.
'Now!' I yelled. 'Now, Trixie—run!'

The taxi was just picking up speed.
Trixie ran fast. She ran straight out
in front of the moving taxi.
The driver hit the brake pedal.
The taxi screeched to a stop.
But Trixie jumped right into the air
and landed on the road in front
of the taxi. She lay on the road
face down, crumpled up.
And she lay quite still.
I prayed she was only acting.

The taxi-driver jumped out of the car
and ran round to Trixie. He bent over her.
'Hey!' he said. 'Are you all right, girl?
Are you all right?'

Trixie lay on the road and didn't move.

'Oh, my God!' the driver cried out.
He ran back to the taxi and grabbed
the mike. 'Hullo, base. Base!
Come in, base. Quick!'

'Base to 32. Base to 32.
What's the trouble, 32?'

'Get the police and ambulance to the
corner of Bell and Crabtree Streets,
Coburg. A girl. I've run over a girl.
It's an emergency. Hurry!'
He threw the mike back into the taxi.

It all happened so quickly from then on.
Lumsden sat in the taxi for a while.
He didn't seem to know what to do.

The taxi-driver ran back to Trixie.
He put his hand on her shoulder
and shook it gently. 'Come on, girl.
Come on. Say something.
Tell me you're all right. Please!'
But Trixie lay quite still on the road.
The orange and blue scarf
clung tightly to her head.

Lumsden got slowly out of the taxi.
He walked round the front and looked
down at the girl. Then he looked
at his watch. He was worried.
He moved over to the taxi-driver
and spoke to him in a low voice.

'But this is an emergency!'
the taxi-driver yelled at Lumsden.
'This girl has been hit!
I can't just leave her on the road!'

Then Lumsden raised his voice.
'Call me another taxi!' he snapped.
'Be quick about it.
I've got a plane to catch.
Hurry, man! Hurry!'

'OK, mister. OK. You watch the girl.'

The taxi-driver ran back to the car
and called another taxi over his radio.
He called out to Lumsden.
'It will be ten minutes
'Bloody hell!' **Lumsden groaned**.

before the other taxi can get here.'

Suddenly I heard the wailing of sirens.
Police? Ambulance? I didn't know.
But Lumsden heard the sirens too.
He quickly muttered something
to the taxi-driver.
Then he grabbed his suitcases from the taxi,
and ran back into the house on the corner.
The wailing sirens grew louder.
Then louder still.

The taxi-driver looked
up and down the street.
He saw me looking round the corner,
but he didn't say anything.
He wasn't worried about *me*.
He was worried about the girl
he had knocked down, and he was watching
for the police and the ambulance.

As soon as I saw the police car,
with its flashing blue light, I raced over
to where Trixie was lying on the road.

The police car screeched round the corner,
and pulled up beside Trixie.

Two policemen jumped out of the car.
'Ambulance is on the way,'
one policeman said. He bent over Trixie.

I tried to tell the other policeman
about Lumsden, but he wouldn't listen.
'A girl's been hurt, son.
Get out of the way.'

By this time quite a few people
had gathered round.
People always seem to appear from nowhere
when there's an accident.

Then Trixie moved.
She turned over on one side and groaned.

'Thank God!' the taxi-driver muttered.
'She's alive! Thank God!'

'Be quiet!' ordered the policeman.
'She's trying to tell me something!'
He bent right down so he could hear Trixie.
Then Trixie started to whisper
in the policeman's ear.
To start with, the policeman frowned.
He looked quickly into Trixie's face.
Then he listened while she whispered
to him again.

Then the ambulance came.
It screamed to a stop
behind the police car.
The policeman beside Trixie jumped up
and spoke quickly to the ambulance men.
The other policeman kept the people,
and me, away from Trixie.

Then one ambulance man went over to
Trixie while the other one got the stretcher
out of the ambulance.

And all the time, I was in a cold sweat
hoping Trixie was really quite OK.

The two policemen spoke together
for a moment. And then the second taxi
arrived—the one Lumsden had ordered.
It pulled up behind the first one,
right outside Lumsden's house.

The two ambulance men were bending
over Trixie. The police were keeping
back the crowd.

But the police saw the second taxi
pull up. The police saw Lumsden creep
out of the house on the corner
and head for the second taxi. So did I.
But the police didn't make a move.
They waited. They waited until Lumsden
had his suitcases in the back of
of that taxi, and they waited until
Lumsden was inside the taxi.

By that time, Trixie had been lifted
on to the stretcher.

Then the police moved.
Lumsden didn't know what had happened
to him. One moment he thought he was
on his way to the airport.
The next moment there were two policemen
standing beside his taxi,
and the ambulance men as well
to back up the police.

And me. And Trixie.

I bet those people in the street
never had such a surprise
as when Trixie jumped off the stretcher
and ran with the ambulance men,
over to the taxi.

Chapter 10

It was Sunday.
The day after Lumsden was caught.
Our living-room was crowded
to over-flowing. First, there were
the two men from the Fisheries and
Wildlife Department. Then there were the
two policemen who had caught Lumsden.
There were five reporters.
There were photographers with flashlights
popping all the time.
There was the poor taxi-driver
who had been so upset
about knocking Trixie down.
There was Mum and Dad.
And Trixie's Mum and Dad.
And there was Trixie and me.

One reporter from a big daily newspaper
wanted to run a front-page story.
He said that the headline could be,

DARING ELEVENTH HOUR TRAP
BY BOY AND GIRL
CRACKS MILLION DOLLAR
SMUGGLING RACKET.

Trixie was flat out talking
  to the reporters.
But I had something else on my mind.
I went up to the men from Fisheries and
Wildlife. 'Hey,' I said to them.
'Can I have my birds back now?
After all, we did get Lumsden for you.'

The men grinned at me.
'Tell you what,' said Mr Hicks.
'You join that bird society,
and we might be able to do something
very special for you.'

'You mean it?' I yelled.

'I mean it, all right,' Mr Hicks said.

'Hey, Trixie!' I yelled across the room.
'We're going to get the birds back!'

Trixie waved to me,
and grinned her special grin.
'That's great!' she called back.
'Then we can risk out lives
on another crazy idea of yours.
Or maybe ruin another birthday present
or two!' She winked at me.

'Get out of it!' I yelled back.
And I grinned at my very favourite
bird of all.